GROWING UP
IN
WORLD WAR II

1941
TO
1945

JUDITH PINKERTON JOSEPHSON

Lerner Publications Company
Minneapolis

To the children of World War II, who knew the truth of Eleanor Roosevelt's words: "This is no ordinary time."

Acknowledgments: Thanks to my manuscript readers: Edith Fine, Bob Jones, and the members of my critique group. For extensive research and help with photos, thanks to Kirsten Josephson, and also the Georgia Historical Society, the Vermont Historical Society, and the Rhode Island Historical Society. For the insights shed on the era, I am grateful to my interview subjects: Jody and Leroy Anderson, Marjorie Greek, Susan Johnson Hadler, Mara Hart, Bob Jones, Fred Landau, and Martha Witz. For her steady guidance, thanks to my editor, Marcia Marshall.

Lerner Publications Company
A division of Lerner Publishing Group, Inc.
241 First Avenue North
Minneapolis, MN 55401 U.S.A.

Website address: www.lernerbooks.com

Photographs and illustrations in this book are used with the permission of:
Franklin D. Roosevelt Library, p. 5 (NLR-PHOCO-66158(10)); © Three Lions/SuperStock, p. 6; © National Archives, pp. 9 (131-NO-9-17, Box 2), 13 (210-62-C153), 24 (NWDNS-210-G-D256), 32 (NWDNS-210-G-A78), 33 (NWDNS-208-NP-3MM-1), 51 (NWDNS-208-N-43888), 52 (W&C 1360); © SuperStock, pp. 10, 36, 38 (top), 40, 42 (top), 55; Susan Johnson Hadler, p. 12 (both); map illustration by Laura Westlund, pp. 14–15; © Brown Brothers, pp. 15, 20, 21, 37, 54, 58; © A.K.G., Berlin/SuperStock, pp. 16, 26, 50; Ruth Berman, p. 17; From the Archives Collection, Birmingham Public Library, Birmingham, Alabama, p. 18; Marjorie Boger Greek, p. 23; C. Leroy and Jody Anderson, pp. 28, 38 (bottom); Nebraska State Historical Society, p. 29; © The Advertising Archive Ltd., pp. 30, 39; Dorinda M. Nicholson, p. 31; The Minnesota Historical Society/The Minneapolis Star-Tribune, p. 34; Bob Jones, p. 35; © Bettmann/CORBIS, pp. 42 (bottom), 43 (top); Mara Kirk Hart, p. 43 (bottom); US Air Force, Courtesy National Air and Space Museum, Smithsonian Institution (SI 91-1471), p. 44; Wilma Briggs, p. 46; Martha Hoffman Witz, pp. 47, 53; Carl Van Vechten Photograph Collection, Library of Congress, p. 48 (LC-USZ62-114554); Lyndon B. Johnson Library, p. 49.

Front cover photo: © Brown Brothers.

Library of Congress Cataloging-in-Publication Data

Josephson, Judith Pinkerton.
    Growing up in World War II, 1941 to 1945 / by Judith Pinkerton Josephson.
        p.   cm. -- (Our America)
    Includes bibliographical references and index.
    ISBN-13: 978–0–8225–0660–7 (lib. bdg. : alk. paper)
    ISBN-10: 0–8225–0660–2 (lib. bdg. : alk. paper)
    1. World War, 1939–1945—Children—United States—Juvenile literature. 2. Children and war—United States--Juvenile literature. 3. United States—Social conditions—1933–1945—Juvenile literature. I. Title: Growing up in World War 2, 1941 to 1945. II. Title: Growing up in World War Two, 1941 to 1945. III. Title. IV. Series.
    D810.C4 J67 2003
    940.53'161--dc21
                                                                                    2002000951

Manufactured in the United States of America
2 3 4 5 6 7 – JR – 12 11 10 09 08 07

CONTENTS

NOTE to READERS

Studying history helps you peek into the past. To find out how people lived in a past time, historians read old diaries and letters. They look at old books, magazines, newspapers, paintings, photographs, and poems. Sometimes they talk with people from that time. All these things are primary sources.

While writing this book, the author used many primary sources. She talked to people who were children and teenagers during World War II. She asked them questions. They told her what their lives were like over sixty years ago. The author also studied articles, letters, posters, movies, slogans, and songs from that era.

Many books about this period are historical fiction. Historical fiction is a made-up story that is set in a real time. You'll find some of these books at the back in Further Reading and Websites.

The people you will meet in this book are real. Even their names—Dorinda, Florence, Jody, Leroy, Marjorie, Martha, Martin, Marialyse, Nancy, Robert,

Many foods were scarce during World War II. Children learned to shop carefully.

Sammy, and Susan—offer clues about the time in which they were young. You'll discover photographs of some of these children. You'll read quotes from their diaries, letters, and memoirs. The quotes are printed just the way they were written, misspellings and all.

As you read, you'll notice many things that are different from modern times, like clothes, customs, and entertainment. You'll also notice some things that are the same.

By studying the primary sources in this book, you can do some snooping of your own. Your ideas about the past will add to our understanding of the people, especially the children, who worked hard on the home front during a time when the world was at war.

CHAPTER ONE

EVERYBODY'S WAR

In 1941 planes from Japan bombed U.S. ships, planes, and buildings
at Pearl Harbor, a U.S. naval base in Hawaii.

"Suddenly we heard the sound of low flying planes, then almost immediately, loud explosions, followed by more planes passing directly over our house."

—*Dorinda Makanaonalani, six, Oahu, Hawaii*

★ ★

On Sunday morning, December 7, 1941, some chilling words blared from radios in Oahu, Hawaii. "Air raid! Pearl Harbor!" the announcer said.

Soldiers rushed to their stations on military bases. Nurses and doctors hurried to the military hospitals. They knew people would be wounded in the surprise attack by Japanese planes.

Dorinda Makanaonalani's family lived in the hills above Pearl Harbor, where the U.S. naval fleet had its base. That Sunday, Dorinda, six, and her father looked up at the planes roaring past their house. Each had a round red sun, Japan's symbol, on the side. Dorinda and her family fled from their home and hid in the sugarcane fields. She had no time to look for her dog, Hula Girl.

"From the cane fields, we could look down and see the harbor on fire," said Dorinda. From their hiding place in the hills, they could see Japanese bombers weaving in and out. Bombs dropped. Torpedos sped underwater. Black smoke billowed. Ships exploded and burned. "I wasn't thinking about the dive bombers . . . I was thinking about my dog, Hula Girl. . . . I knew she was scared with all of the noisy blasts and explosions."

That day, Ginger, a teenager living on an air force base in Hawaii, wrote in her diary: "BOMBED!. . . We've left the post. . . . The PX [store] is in flames, also the barracks. . . . Left everything we own. . . . I can't believe it's really happening. It's awful. School is discontinued until further notice. . . . There goes my graduation."

"I wasn't thinking about the dive bombers . . . I was thinking about my dog, Hula Girl. . . ."

—*Dorinda Makanaonalani*

The attack had damaged or destroyed twenty-one ships, three hundred planes, and many homes and cars. Almost 2,400 people had died, with 2,000 more wounded. In a radio address to the nation, America's president, Franklin D. Roosevelt, called the day of the attack a "date which will live in infamy [evil]."

Dorinda and her family slept on the floor of a sugarcane factory for several days. Finally they returned home. Stray bullets had lodged in the kitchen walls. Fire had singed the roof. Dorinda found Hula Girl under the house, whimpering. The dog was weak, but her tail was wagging.

★ ★ ★ ★

"WE CAN DO IT!"

Slowly, people learned details from the radio, newspapers, magazines, and movie newsreels. (Television wasn't available then.) A wave of patriotic spirit swept over the country. The government (nicknamed Uncle Sam) urged people to support the war. Children could help, too—at school, at home, or in their communities.

Aldolf Hitler's plan was to rule the world.

EVERYBODY'S WAR

A few years before Pearl Harbor, war had begun in Europe. Germany's leader, Adolf Hitler, had sent his Nazi troops into nearby countries. He was carrying out his plan to rule the world with his pure "German master race" and to kill Jews and others he thought were "inferior." One by one, the other nations of Europe began to oppose him. Some countries joined his cause.

Many American children had helped collect clothing for war refugees in Europe. They had seen pictures of bombed-out buildings. Connecticut farm girl Nancy Potter, fifteen, had an English pen pal. The English girl had spent many nights in a London bomb shelter to escape the German bombing. She wrote Nancy all about it.

After the attack on Pearl Harbor, the United States joined forces with Great Britain, France, and the Soviet Union to fight Germany, Italy, and Japan. World War II had become everybody's war.

★ ★ ★ ★

EYES ON THE ENEMY

To prepare for a possible air attack, many cities held air raid drills at night. Windows had to be covered with light-blocking shades or curtains. This way, enemy planes flying overhead wouldn't be able to see where to drop bombs. People also covered their car headlights with tape, leaving only a slit for light.

Postal workers and military officers opened and checked the mail. Dorinda Makanaonalani's father worked at the Oahu post office. Workers there censored letters by blacking out or cutting out any words that might help the enemy, such as clues to where troops were stationed or where they might be headed.

★ ★ ★ ★

"THERE'S WORK TO BE DONE AND A WAR TO BE WON!"

Many men, ages eighteen to thirty-six, left their factory jobs and joined the armed forces. Women and some older teenagers took their places.

U.S. factories stopped making toasters, toys, bicycles, typewriters, cars, and other everyday items. Within months, these companies switched to making weapons, tanks, airplanes, and other war supplies.

Children soon understood what this meant. Dot Chastney's father had promised her a two-wheel bicycle when she turned eight. Then factories stopped making bicycles. Dot was heartbroken.

These women are building a plane. Many women did this kind of work during the war.

* * * *

"Loose Lips Sink Ships!"

The government had warned Americans to watch what they said and to be on the lookout for spies. Some people grew suspicious of friends or neighbors who were Japanese, German, or Italian. On the Rosebud Sioux Indian Reservation in South Dakota, Robert Raymond, ten, looked for spies. "All people with German-sounding names were suspect. Lucky for me, I never was able to find one."

> *"All people with German-sounding names were suspect."*
> — *Robert Raymond, ten*

At Leroy Anderson's school in Idaho, an "invisible line" separated Japanese American students from their white classmates. Friendships became awkward.

America's military leaders went even further to protect Americans from what they saw as a threat. In the spring of 1942, President Roosevelt ordered 110,000 Japanese Americans on the West Coast to leave their homes and go to live at relocation, or internment, camps. Many were American citizens. One out of five were children.

Jeanne Wakatsuki, age seven, was sent to Manzanar (a California relocation center) with her mother and nine brothers and sisters.

WAR ORPHANS

Susan Johnson *(top right)* was born during the war. Her father, Dave S. Johnson Jr. *(bottom right)*, twenty-five, served as a U.S. soldier in Europe. He wrote her a letter from France:

> Dear Susan,
> Since I can't be there in person this is a sort of "welcome" letter. Yours is a pretty good family. . . . Your dad is a bit on the off-side, but your mother and brother and now you, more than make up for that.
>
> Your brother is quite a guy—of course, he's quite handsome and smart—will he get around—but I know he'll always be ready to guide you and protect you in every way.
> Your mother is the most wonderful person I've ever known. I've always marveled at my great good fortune to have loved her and been loved by her. If you will follow her dictates and examples, you may expect to meet life in the best possible way and your path will always be the right one. . . .
>
> For me, adhere to a belief in tolerance, a genuine liking for others, and always give to life to the fullest.
> Your father,
> Dave

Soon after writing this letter, Susan's father died in a land mine explosion. Susan and her older brother became war orphans (children who lost one or both parents in the war).

After the Japanese bombed Pearl Harbor, Japanese Americans were sent away from their homes to relocation camps. Families wore identification tags around their necks.

Jeanne's father had lived in America for thirty-five years. The government accused him of delivering oil to Japanese submarines and sent him to a detention center. He rejoined his family a year later, but he had become a sad, angry man. "This was the beginning of a terrible, frantic time for all my family," said Jeanne.

★ ★ ★ ★

BAD GUYS VS. GOOD GUYS

World War II became part of many children's play, work, school, and thoughts. Many families tacked world maps on the wall. They marked battle lines with colored pins.

Movies, books, newsreels, and cartoons told Americans they must be patriotic. The bad guys were the Germans, the Italians, and the Japanese. The good guys were the Soviets, the British, and the Americans.

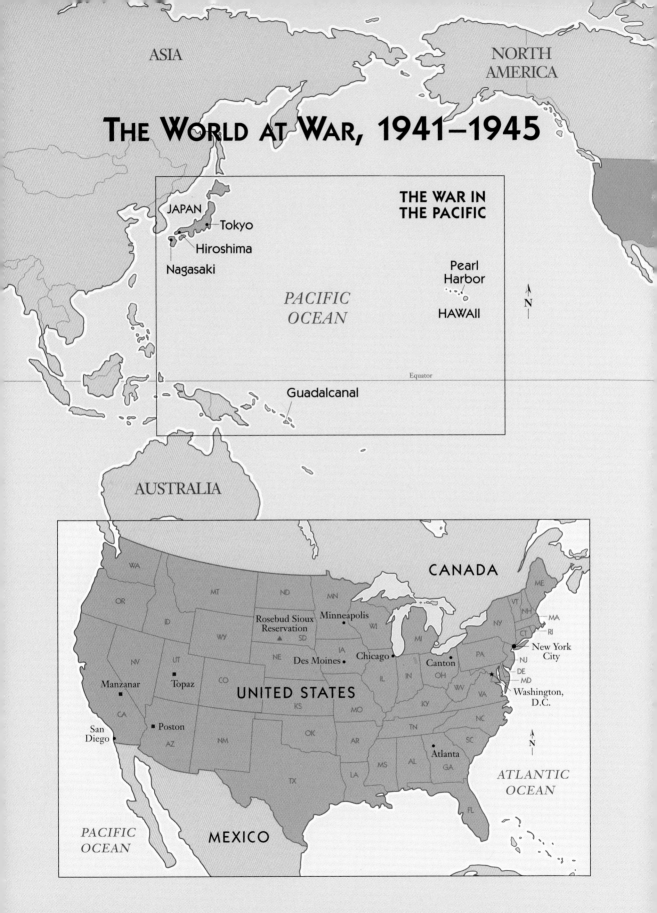

THE WORLD AT WAR, 1941–1945

ASIA

NORTH AMERICA

THE WAR IN THE PACIFIC

JAPAN

Tokyo

Hiroshima

Nagasaki

PACIFIC OCEAN

Pearl Harbor

HAWAII

N

Equator

Guadalcanal

AUSTRALIA

CANADA

WA

OR

MT

ND

MN

ME

VT

NH

ID

WY

SD

Rosebud Sioux Reservation

Minneapolis

WI

NY

MA

RI

CT

NV

UT

NE

IA

MI

PA

NJ

DE

MD

Manzanar

Topaz

CO

Des Moines

Chicago

IL

IN

OH

Canton

WV

VA

Washington, D.C.

New York City

CA

San Diego

Poston

KS

MO

KY

NC

TN

SC

UNITED STATES

AZ

NM

OK

AR

MS

AL

Atlanta

GA

N

TX

LA

FL

ATLANTIC OCEAN

PACIFIC OCEAN

MEXICO

THE WAR
IN EUROPE

GREAT
BRTAIN

NORWAY

DENMARK

NETHERLANDS
LUXEMBOURG
BELGIUM GERMANY
FRANCE

EUROPE

ITALY

SOVIET
UNION
(RUSSIA)

ATLANTIC
OCEAN

UNITED STATES
(see inset,
bottom left)

Axis Control

Allied Countries

Neutral Countries

AFRICA

SOUTH
AMERICA

Americans listened to
President Roosevelt's regular
"fireside chats" on the radio.
Not everybody liked
Roosevelt, but Americans
united behind him and the
war effort. Many young
people agreed with Marialyse
Hager, age fourteen: "To
those of us in that age group,
Roosevelt was. . . going to
make the world safe for us."

President Franklin D. Roosevelt's radio "fireside
chats" helped Americans feel safe.

Other young people weren't so sure about the future. On New
Year's Eve, 1941, after her family left Hawaii for the mainland,
Ginger, age seventeen, wrote in her diary, "Well, 1941 goes off rather
in the way of making history. . . I for one will never forget it. We are
all going to bed early, as usual. . . . Happy New Year? I wonder."

CHAPTER TWO

TOGETHER FOR VICTORY

MORE PRODUCTION EVERY HOUR—
GIVES OUR FORCES GREATER POWER

DEAR
POPPA

"Dear Poppa,

I think you are like Abraham Lincoln. . . .

I love you very much and I'm very proud

of you. . . . "

—*Sammy Berman, six, Minneapolis, Minnesota, May 5, 1944*

★ ★

Reuben Berman, a Minneapolis doctor, was stationed in Europe during the war. Like other children whose fathers were away, his son Sammy, six, worried. In one letter, Sammy warned his father: "There's such a thing as a rocket. A rocket is a great big bullet with a machine in it and if it hits you you'll die."

Sammy Berman, age six

★ ★ ★ ★

CITY LIFE

Mara Hart and Bob Jones were six when the war began. Both had grandmothers who lived with their families. Mara's family lived in a New York City apartment. Bob Jones's family rented a small, two-bedroom house in Des Moines, Iowa. His mother worked in a weapons factory that once had made tractors.

In Iowa, winters are long and cold. Coal, which was burned to keep houses warm, was scarce during the war. Without coal for heat, frigid outdoor air would seep into the house. "When the coal bin started to grow empty, it was scary—it meant we might run out," said Bob.

"When the coal bin started to grow empty, it was scary—it meant we might run out,"

— Bob Jones

Martha Hoffman, a teenager, lived in Mount Vernon, New York, a suburb of New York City. Her family was poor, but nobody went hungry. Martha's mother had a vegetable garden and kept a cow and chickens.

African American Martin Luther King Jr. was twelve when America joined the war. He lived in Atlanta, Georgia. Martin's father and grandfather were ministers, so family life centered on the church.

In many southern states, African Americans faced segregation (enforced separation of people by race) every day.

In many parts of America, especially the South, African Americans couldn't go to the same theaters, schools, and other public places that white people went to. Martin couldn't go to the same school or ride on the same part of the bus as his white friends.

COUNTRY LIFE

Leroy Anderson grew up on a small Idaho farm. At night, after chores and homework, his family told stories and talked. The Andersons had no radio. They learned the news from neighbors. The family owned only three big books—the Bible, *The People's Home Library*, and Leroy's favorite, *The People's War Book and Atlas*.

Robert Raymond's parents had died when he was young. So he and his ten brothers and sisters lived with his oldest sister near Mission, South Dakota, on the Rosebud Reservation. An older brother, Jack, was a soldier. He sent letters to his family from where he was stationed in Africa and Europe. Robert sent Jack a picture of Partner, the family dog. Jack wrote back:

> *Sept. 8, 1943*
> *North Africa*
> *Dear Bobby,*
> *Sure was glad to hear from you on your new stationery. . . .*
> *Wished you'd write more often . . . I'm sending [paper money]*
> *for souvenirs . . . tell everyone "hello" for me, including*
> *Partner. . . .*
> *With love,*
> *your brother,*
> *Jack*

★ ★ ★ ★

"FOOD IS A WEAPON! DON'T WASTE IT!"

The war changed what people ate. Feeding the American troops took massive amounts of food, so the government limited how much sugar, butter, and meat families could buy. Sugar was the first item to be rationed (limited). That meant fewer sweets. Next came coffee,

During World War II, the government rationed gasoline.
People purchased it with gas ration coupons like these.

cooking oil, and canned and fresh meat, fish, and chicken. Gasoline and tires, needed for military vehicles, were rationed, too.

Each person received a ration book filled with coupons. Rationed items cost a certain number of coupons. When coupons ran out for the week or month, people did without or used substitutes, like oleomargarine for butter. Florence Fleming, eight, hated ice cream made with soybean flour instead of sugar. "Urp! Phooey-p'tooie!" she said.

Children helped plant and harvest vegetable gardens in backyards, vacant lots, and city parks. These were called victory gardens. This "Grow Your Own, Can Your Own!" idea spread until twenty million victory gardens were producing almost half of the nation's fruits and vegetables.

Jody Rhoads's family owned a large Wyoming cattle ranch. She often played with her cousin Bob, whose father was away in the war. On the Rhoads' ranch, fifty hens and two milk cows supplied the family with plenty of eggs, butter, and cream. Jody's mother traded some of her butter and egg coupons for her neighbors' sugar coupons. She had a special reason. Four of her brothers were in the war, and they loved homemade caramel candy. Jody helped her mother make boxes of sweet caramels to send to her uncles. "Mom would stand for

Children water plants and harvest peas in a community victory garden.

hours and stir and stir each rich, bubbling mass," Jody said. " She and I would wrap and wrap and wrap each special nugget in waxed paper."

★ ★ ★ ★

"USE IT UP, WEAR IT OUT, MAKE IT DO, OR DO WITHOUT!"

People made do with the clothes they had. Women's skirts grew shorter and narrower. Men's trousers came without cuffs to save material. People lined shoes with cardboard to cover holes in the soles or bought replacement soles to glue onto the bottoms of old shoes. In Hawaii, stores often ran out of toilet paper. Dorinda Makanaonalani's mother rubbed pieces of newspaper together to soften them. "That became our toilet paper," said Dorinda.

People kept old cars running, hoping they'd last until the war ended. For most families, traveling by bus or streetcar replaced traveling by car. When people did drive, they drove more slowly to save gas. Signs asked, "Is This Trip Really Necessary?"

★ ★ ★ ★

FAMILIES ON THE MOVE

From 1942 to 1945, almost five million families moved. Young John E. Smith's family moved to California, where there were many wartime jobs. John's mother drove a military tow truck. His grandparents and aunt worked in an airplane factory. John's father was in England, hauling fuel for the army.

Each Friday night, the Smiths gathered around the radio to listen to the war news. No talking was allowed. John remembered "seeing faces so serious that I was afraid."

★ ★ ★ ★

BLACKOUTS AND AIR RAID DRILLS

Cities on both coasts had air raid drills (practice for what to do in case enemy planes bombed American targets). Both Mara Hart's parents were air raid wardens (leaders) in New York City. Once a week, the air raid siren blew. Mara's parents grabbed their helmets, flashlights, and badges. Like other air raid wardens, they hurried citizens off the streets and made sure no lights could be seen.

THE GOLD STAR NOBODY WANTED

Families hung a banner with a blue star in their windows for each family member in the military. A gold star meant the relative had died. Florence Fleming's cousin had married a young U.S. Air Force officer. When the family's star changed from blue to gold in the summer of 1943, Florence knew the worst had happened. "I hated the war even more," she said.

SOMEONE NEW AT MARJORIE'S HOUSE

When Marjorie Boger was eight, a ten-year-old English girl, Vina Wales, came to live with Marjorie's family in North Canton, Ohio. Many English families sent their children to Canada and the United States so they would be safe from the war in Europe. At Vina's first meal with the Boger family, she ran from the room, crying. Marjorie's mother comforted the homesick child.

Over the next five years, Vina became part of Marjorie's family. The girls called each others' parents "aunt" and "uncle." Marjorie and her sister introduced Vina to eating hot dogs and ice cream cones, and to other American customs.

Marjorie *(standing)*, her sister Elaine *(left)*, and Vina Wales

Mara, her sister Kitty, and their grandmother covered the windows with blackout shades so no light from the house was visible from the street or sky. The girls filled the bathtub with water, in case the water supply was cut off. Then they grabbed their flashlights, turned out the lights, and sat in the long, dark hallway.

Mara worried about her mother during these drills. "My mother would go into Morningside Park alone," said Mara. "Life seemed very tentative, very dark." Once the "all clear" siren sounded, Mara's parents came home. Life returned to normal—until sirens blared again.

> *"Life seemed very tentative, very dark."*
>
> — *Mara Hart, ten*

FAMILY LIFE IN THE INTERNMENT CAMPS

Japanese Americans ordered to relocate were sent to live in camps in the West and South. Most families had little time to get ready to move. They left their homes, family heirlooms, and pets behind.

Often, people showed kindness to Japanese neighbors who were forced to move. Some volunteered to protect their belongings while they were away. Clara Breed, a San Diego librarian, gave her young patrons stamped postcards. She asked them to write to her from camp. Many did. Louise Ogawa, seventeen, wrote the librarian about No. 3 camp in Poston, Arizona. "It is so sandy that everyone's hair looks gray. . . . There is no water on Sundays."

At the relocation centers, Japanese American families lived in rooms with few pieces of furniture.

The U.S. government had prepared ten internment camps for the families. Barbed wire and armed guards surrounded most of them. In one temporary camp at a racetrack, each family lived in a horse stall.

At Manzanar in California, in warm weather, people left the crowded barracks and spent their time outside. Jeanne Wakatsuki remembered: "You only went home at night, when you finally had to."

At Manzanar only the camp laundry had running water. People stood in line to use smelly latrines (toilets) with no doors or walls between seats. Jeanne's mother never got used to the latrines. "It was a humiliation she just learned to endure." Inside the barracks, flimsy dividers separated the "rooms," lighted by a single lightbulb.

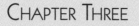

Chapter Three

Uncle Sam Wants You!

"We're doin' war work. It's our war, just as much—or maybe more—than anybody else's."

—Annie, ("Little Orphan Annie" comic strip character), 1942

★ ★ ★ ★ ★ ★ ★ ★ ★ ★ ★ ★ ★ ★ ★ ★ ★ ★ ★ ★

Little Orphan Annie, a comic strip character, wanted children to do real war work, like buying war stamps and collecting scrap metal for making war supplies. In youth groups like the Boy Scouts and Girl Scouts, children rolled bandages and collected milkweed pods. (The silky floss inside was used to stuff life jackets.) Both boys and girls knitted squares to be sewn together for blankets for soldiers.

★ ★ ★ ★

HOME CHORES AND ODD JOBS

At home, children helped by doing chores, like setting the table and washing dishes. Another job was squeezing the capsule of yellow coloring into oleomargarine, a butter substitute. Oleo was pure white and came in a clear cellophane package. Adding the yellow coloring made it look more like butter.

"Many Friday nights were spent around the kitchen table, kneading and mixing the white stuff into butter-looking stuff," said Dorinda Makanaonalani.

Starting at age ten, Mara Hart ironed her family's clothes. It took Mara four hours to finish one week's ironing.

When Martin Luther King Jr. was eleven, he helped tend the furnace. He wrote his parents, who were away on church business:

HOME ALONE

With both men and women working, many children stayed at home with other adults. A babysitter stayed with Gary Paulsen, age five, while his mother worked in a Chicago ammunitions plant. Gary's father was overseas. When Gary grew up, he became a famous writer of books for young people. One of his books, *Cookcamp*, is about a WWII child. Other children of working parents stayed with relatives, went to child care centers, or stayed home alone.

"I am keeping the fire burning but Mr. Gibson had to put some coal in the basement because it gave out." Martin also did extra jobs to earn money for his family. During the summers, he ran a soft drink stand. He also delivered the *Atlanta Journal*. "I am being a good boy," he wrote. "I made 35c. off my paper this week and have some more to collect."

★ ★ ★ ★

"GET YOUR FARM IN THE FIGHT"

Farms and ranches that produced goods and food aided the war effort. In the South, cotton farmers planted extra cotton. It took 250 pounds of cotton to make one soldier's socks, uniforms, underwear, sheets, and pillowcases. On some farms, women and children did all the work, because men and older boys had gone to war. On ranches, even young children helped herd cattle. "I was in the saddle as soon as I could stay on top of a horse and follow a cow," said Jody Rhoads.

Jody Rhoads *(right)* and her cousin Bob ride Princey on the Rhoads' family ranch.

★ ★ ★ ★

"Kids Out A-Pickin' Spuds"

America's need for soldiers and factory workers had left larger farms short of field hands. Children helped keep these farms running. Young people worked the dusty rows, digging potatoes. For each gunnysack filled, they earned ten cents. After hours of digging potatoes, Robert Stout, age eleven, said, "I was too tired to straighten as I moved from one clump to another . . . my knuckles dragging the dirt, my eyes squinting up at the sun, as I wished it were five o'clock."

To save gasoline, people used mules or horses to pull farm machines or did chores by hand. One slogan was, "Lend Him a Hand, Do It by Hand." Working with a horse-drawn cultivator, Robert Stout carefully stepped around steaming piles of horse manure as he harvested potatoes. Robert's father had also planted one thousand onion plants in the family's garden plot. While weeding them, Robert imagined himself dodging enemy planes and saving lives.

To conserve gasoline, some dairies and other businesses went back to using horse-drawn vehicles to make deliveries.

UNCLE SAM'S NIECES AND NEPHEWS

"Uncle Sam is asking his sturdy young nephews and nieces to serve on the home front," announced a New Jersey agency in 1942. Some 12,000 young people planted and harvested fruit, peas, spinach, and onions. This summer work earned the young people about one dollar a day.

In Oregon 270,000 students, ages eleven to seventeen, became Victory Farm Volunteers. They grew beans, raspberries, beets, and strawberries in the summers. Other teens worked in plants that canned fruits and vegetables. Japanese American teens from the relocation camps in western states helped harvest sugar beets. But some town folks refused to serve these teens in local restaurants.

ROSIE THE RIVETER

Thousands of women and older teenage girls learned how to do carpentry and electrical work and how to weld, rivet, and solder, just like men. Being paid for these new skills gave female workers confidence. Workers like Mary Wilderhain, eighteen, felt that they, too, were fighting for their country.

Rosie the Riveter became the symbol of this new, female workforce. The real-life worker behind this national symbol was Rosina Bonavits. Rosie and

J. Howard Miller designed this poster of Rosie the Riveter.

a female coworker had put 3,345 rivets on a fighter airplane wing in only six hours. Rosie appeared on posters, her hair tied in a bandana, her arm flexed. "We Can Do It!" said Rosie.

★ ★ ★ ★

SCHOOL DURING THE WAR

America's schools kept reminding children of the war, with victory assemblies, victory sings, and parades. Students learned the marching songs of all the armed forces.

During drills at Mara Hart's school, students practiced what to do if a real air raid happened. "The boys sat under certain tables, the girls under certain tables. . . . It was a giggling time. Everything seemed safe and funny during the day. It was the nights that were scary."

In the Hawaiian Islands, everybody carried gas masks because people worried that the Japanese might attack again. They might even use poison gas. Dorinda Makanaonalani and her brother Ishmael carried gas masks to school.

> *"Everything seemed safe and funny during the day. It was the nights that were scary."*
> —*Mara Hart, ten*

Dorinda and her brother Ishmael pose in the gas masks they had to take to school in Hawaii.

★ ★ ★ ★

CLASSROOM LIFE

In rural areas, youngsters like Leroy Anderson and Jody Rhoads still went to one-room schoolhouses. From sixteen to thirty-five children attended grades one through eight. Students read war news in the *Weekly Reader*, a classroom newspaper.

Most children attended larger elementary schools, then went on to high school. Some cities also had junior high schools for grades seven and eight. Despite the war, Martin Luther King Jr. took studying seriously. He skipped two grades in high school and entered Morehouse College at age fifteen.

"AMERICA"

Typical school days started with "The Pledge of Allegiance." Students sang a patriotic song, such as "America," which begins, "My country 'tis of thee, sweet land of liberty." This song first became popular during the Civil War (1861–1865).

Schoolchildren in San Francisco, California, recite "The Pledge of Allegiance."

In 1943 public schoolchildren in the south-central district of Chicago, Illinois, bought enough war bonds and stamps to buy 125 jeeps, 2 pursuit planes, and a motorcycle.

★ ★ ★ ★

"WE WON'T LET YOU DOWN!"

A nationwide program, called Schools at War, urged children to save, serve, and conserve. Children could save by buying war stamps and bonds. "They are flying 'em [planes]; we should buy 'em. Ten Cents Every Day in War Bonds!" was one slogan. Stamps cost ten cents, and with a filled book of stamps, you could purchase a war bond. Sixth graders at one Kansas school raised $331.15. Their war bond bought one submachine gun, four field telephones, one tent, five steel helmets, and nine tools for digging trenches.

To serve, children could make war posters, work at child care centers, and tend victory gardens. One group of Florida schoolchildren grew enough vegetables to feed the whole school at lunchtime.

To conserve, children collected newspapers, cooking fat, and scrap metal. Metal foil peeled off gum wrappers and cigarette packages

Kids in Minneapolis, Minnesota, supported the war effort by collecting scrap aluminum.

was rolled into five-pound balls. Students hauled flattened tin cans, pans, coins, keys, and nails to school. One Kansas boy added his prized red-and-white pedal car to the pile. Chicago schoolchildren collected 1.5 million pounds of scrap metal. When melted down, one lawn mower made six big artillery shells. An iron became thirty hand grenades. Kitchen fats and grease were used in bombs, medicines, and synthetic rubber.

The United States's main source for rubber, the Far East, was under Japanese control. Children helped collect old rubber raincoats, garden hoses, and tires. Rubber goods could be remade into tires for military tanks, trucks, and planes.

★ ★ ★ ★

SCHOOLS BEHIND BARBED WIRE

In the Japanese American relocation camps, classrooms were crowded. Students often shared textbooks. Hisako Watanabe, seventeen, commented: "When school started three months ago there were no chairs, tables or books. . . . Everyone had their father or brother make them a chair." Children carried these crude chairs to school.

In 1942 in a camp near Topaz, Utah, Lillian "Anne" Yamauchi had her third-graders keep a diary. On March 11, 1943, they noted, "Yesterday we started to join the American Junior Red Cross. Please

SCHOOL CLOTHES

Mara Hart and her sister Kitty walked to elementary school. If the temperature fell below 32°F, their mother made them wear long cotton stockings under their skirts.

"We hated those stockings," said Mara. On cold mornings, she or Kitty held their finger on the thermometer until the temperature rose above 32°F, so that they wouldn't have to wear them. Fred Landau also hated what he wore to school—itchy wool knickers (knee-length pants worn with high socks).

In junior high, many girls wore plaid skirts with sweaters. Sometimes dickeys were tucked inside the sweaters. Dickeys were garments that looked like blouses but were just collars attached to enough fabric to stay put. Girls wore saddle shoes or penny loafers with heavy, white bobby socks.

remember to put 10% of your pay into war bonds and stamps. We should not kill spiders because Uncle Sam needs them for the war." The silky strands of spiderwebs were used to form the crosshairs in airplane bombsights. These tiny crossed lines helped soldiers aim bombs dropped on enemy targets.

Some school days, the war seemed far away. When Bob Jones and classmate Gertrude Glazer scored the top grades in their class, their teacher let them skip school and go to the movies. Bob and Gertrude watched a newsreel and the feature film *Phantom of the Opera*.

Bob Jones *(right)*, ten, with his older brother Ron, twelve

CHAPTER FOUR

COMMANDOS
and
SUPERHEROES

"Nothing could compare with the thrill of skating up one street and down another, with the wind in your hair."

—*Martha Hoffman, fifteen, Mount Vernon, New York*

★ ★

Despite the war, children found ways to have fun. Martha Hoffman loved roller-skating and jumping rope. "Some days, we jump roped from nine in the morning until dark," said Martha.

Fred Landau and his friends played stickball, a game like baseball. To play, they only needed a broom handle, a tennis ball, and a city street.

Bob Jones and his friends played cards and competed in Ping-Pong and marble tournaments. Kids walked everywhere—to school,

In fair weather, roller-skating was popular. Children wore metal skates over their shoes. The skates were tightened into place with a key.

to the library, to the park. During snowy Iowa winters, children sledded down slopes and along snow-packed streets. Children without sleds used cardboard or slid on their feet.

It hardly ever snowed in Atlanta, Georgia, where Martin Luther King Jr. lived. But after one rare winter snowstorm, Martin wrote, "We are really having a fine time makeing snowmen and throwing snow balls."

In winter children sledded down snowy hills.

★ ★ ★ ★

PLAYING WAR

In Idaho Leroy Anderson daydreamed about being a fighter pilot. "My make-believe firing was always from behind a rock, a stump," he said. "I also imagined that I was wounded . . . but I never imagined

Leroy Anderson *(upper right)* with his fifth, sixth, and seventh grade classmates in Idaho.

"My make-believe firing was always from behind a rock. . . . I also imagined that I was wounded . . . but I never imagined that I might be killed. . . ."
—*Leroy Anderson*

that I might be killed. . . . In the air, I pictured myself in full military uniform, flying a P-39 Airacobra or P-51 Mustang [fighter planes]."

Jody Rhoads and her cousin Bob played commandos, named after military hit-and-run units. In the barnyard, the cousins shot at imaginary enemies. They built dugouts and barriers out of woven wire and leaves. They walked along fences and shinnied up and down the hay feeder.

Because Robert Raymond's brother was a soldier, Robert knew all about tanks, guns, hand grenades, and jeeps. He memorized soldiers' ranks. Robert was proud of his brother when he was promoted to the rank of sergeant.

★ ★ ★ ★

RADIO'S GOLDEN AGE

Organ music and a creaking door announced radio's *Inner Sanctum*, a popular mystery series. Each show began with the announcer saying, "Good evening, friends of the inner sanctum. . . . This is your host to welcome you . . . into the land of ghosts and vampires."

On another show, Captain Midnight told children, "You are the keen-eyed fliers of tomorrow. . . . the skippers of atomic-powered ships. . . . America needs you—healthy, alert, and well trained to guard her future."

The most popular western adventure show was *The Lone Ranger*. The Lone Ranger was a masked man who rode a white horse named Silver. Tonto, his Native

Families listened to the radio together. Radios brought them war news, as well as mystery and action programs.

American partner, was never far away. Children listened for the Lone Ranger's familiar words, "Hi-Yo, Silver! Away!"

Cowboy and Indian movies usually favored the cowboys. Robert Raymond and his friend, Doley White Eyes, watched a movie in which Buffalo Bill Cody killed a Cheyenne warrior, Yellow Hand. Doley's mother let the boys know that the movie didn't tell the whole story from the Native American point of view.

★ ★ ★ ★

SUPERHEROES

Superheroes all had double identities. They led ordinary lives until they switched to fighting villains and doing good works. Many children could imagine having similar strength and powers.

The Adventures of Superman radio show began, "Faster than a speeding bullet! More powerful than a locomotive! Able to leap tall buildings at a single bound! . . . It's a bird! It's a plane! It's Superman!"

Most superheroes were men. But in 1941, Wonder Woman appeared. Smart, strong, and fast, Wonder Woman caught evildoers with her golden lariat (rope). Her gold bracelets

At last a female superhero: Wonder Woman!

stopped speeding bullets. Finally girls had a superhero too. Wonder Woman relied on herself, not on men.

★ ★ ★ ★
HOLLYWOOD GOES TO WAR

In 1942 the movie *Mrs. Miniver* won an Academy Award. In the movie, an English family endured bombing raids and deaths of family and friends. *Mrs. Miniver* helped convince many Americans, especially young people, that this was "the people's war," worth dying for.

Neal Shine, eleven when the war began, remembered that war movies made kids feel part of key battles: "We were on Guadalcanal, we were in *Thirty Seconds over Tokyo*, we were carried away to these places." In one movie, Neal's friend got so excited that he threw a golf ball at the screen to stop the approaching Japanese troops. "All he did was mess up the screen," said Neal. *Thirty Seconds over Tokyo* told the true story of war hero Lieutenant Colonel James Doolittle and his daring bombing raid over Japan.

★ ★ ★ ★
NANCY DREW AND THE HARDY BOYS

Martha Hoffman and her cousins and friends competed to see who could read the most books. Classic books included *Mary Poppins, Lassie Come-Home, The Adventures of Huckleberry Finn, Little Women,* and *Treasure Island.* Popular book series for girls were the Bobbsey Twins and Nancy Drew mysteries. Boys loved the Hardy Boys and Tom Swift books.

★ ★ ★ ★
COMIC BOOKS

During the war years, children bought twenty million comic books a

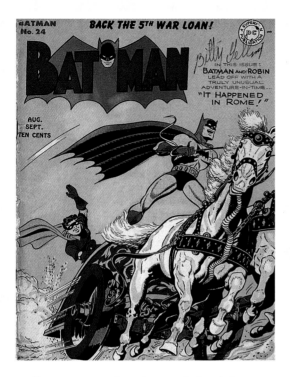

Batman was a favorite comic book hero.

month. Favorites were Popeye, Bugs Bunny, Mickey Mouse, Superman, Batman, and Archie.

Many cartoon strips for children had war-related plots. Popeye urged readers: "Let's blast 'em Japanazis!" Little Orphan Annie wanted all kids to become Junior Commandos. On the cover of a July 1942 Walt Disney comic book,

BATON TWIRLING THE AMERICAN WAY

After three years in the Manzanar Relocation Camp, Jeanne Wakatsuki took up baton twirling. She practiced with a sawed-off broomstick that had an old tennis ball stuck on one end. "Baton twirling was one trick I could perform that was thoroughly, unmistakenly American, putting on the boots and a dress crisscrossed with braid, spinning the silver stick and tossing it high to the tune of a John Philip Sousa march," said Jeanne.

The Slinky®, inspired by an accident, became a popular toy.

Goofy and Donald Duck carried an American flag.

★ ★ ★ ★

War Toys

In 1943 a spring fell to the deck of a U.S. naval ship and bounced around. That gave engineer Richard James an idea. He and his wife made a coil of lightweight steel that bounced, wriggled, and slithered. James called this new toy a Slinky ®. Kids loved it.

Another engineer's recipe for a rubber substitute didn't work. The stuff bounced and erased like rubber but broke apart easily. Thinking kids might like his invention, he called it Gooey Gupp. Later it became Silly Putty® and was sold in red plastic eggs. Thirty-two million eggs sold in the first five years.

Not all children had as many toys as some modern children do. "It's amazing how little we needed to have fun," said Mara Hart.

Mara Hart (left) and her sister Kitty enjoyed playing with their dogs.

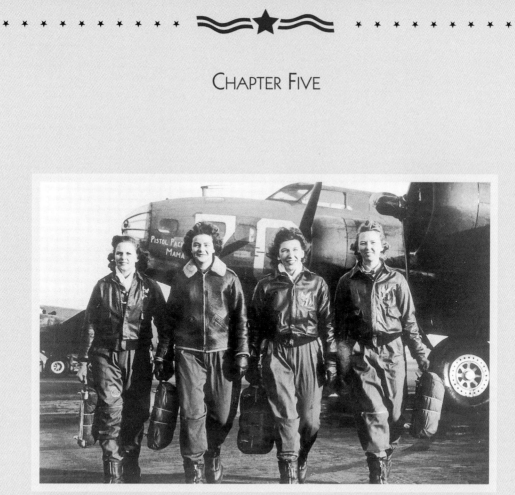

CHAPTER FIVE

CHANGING LIVES

Four WASPS (Women's Air Force Service Pilots) stride off to work in their flight suits.

"I cannot imagine a day that I spent, from the time I was 14 until I was 19, that I wasn't aware of the war . . . it had an impact on everything I chose to do."

—Nancy Potter, Connecticut teen

★ ★

For some young people, war made the future seem uncertain. Others found it exciting. In Tennessee, John Wells and his friends often gathered at Mack's Grocery. A poster said: "Join the Navy, See the World, Learn a Trade!" Just fifteen, John Wells lied about his age, forged his parents' signature, and joined the Navy. He weighed only 106 pounds.

On the Sioux Reservation in South Dakota, where he lived, Robert Raymond listened to the war news and studied the newspaper. "I was very afraid for my brother, but I didn't know how or what I could do to help him," said Robert.

Women could not fight in combat the way men did. But at twenty or twenty-one, they could join special branches of the services, like the Women's Army Corps (WACs), the Women's Air Force Service Pilots (WASPs), and the WAVES, the women's naval group.

Eileen Hughes was too young for any of these. Instead she joined the Civil Air Patrol in Rhode Island. At observation posts, spotters like Eileen scanned the skies and offshore waters, looking for enemy airplanes, ships, and submarines.

THE GIRL WHO LOVED BASEBALL

Connecticut farm girl Wilma Briggs loved baseball. Because of World War II, she got the chance to play professional baseball. Three-fourths of baseball's professional players had joined the armed services, including star players like Joe DiMaggio and Jackie Robinson. To keep baseball fans happy, the All-American Girls' Professional Baseball League formed in 1943. After high school, Wilma Briggs joined the league and traveled all over the country. Later Wilma went to college and became a schoolteacher.

"BE WITH HIM AT EVERY MAIL CALL"

Young people often wrote to the boys overseas. "We were constantly writing to boost soldiers' morale," said Nancy Potter. Some girls pressed lipstick kisses on the backs of V-Mails, written on thin blue paper. The V stood for victory. All six of Marialyse Hager's brothers were fighting in the war. She saw the worry on her mother's face when she wrote them.

For many girls, writing letters took the place of dating. "We were always interested in dating," said Mary Wilderhain. "We just couldn't find anyone to date!"

"We were always interested in dating. We just couldn't find anyone to date!"

— *Mary Wilderhain, teenager*

★ ★ ★ ★

"A HOME AWAY FROM HOME: THE USO"

In many towns, soldiers on leave or stationed nearby went to the United
Service Organization (USO). Here older girls served food and talked
and danced with lonely soldiers. New York City's USO served dinner
every night. An orchestra played. "It was the greatest thing that could
have happened to the female population," said Martha Hoffman. "I
had a ball."

★ ★ ★ ★

AMERICA'S COLOR BAR

In the Japanese relocation camps, teenagers and their families felt
like prisoners even though they had done nothing wrong. Louise

Martha Hoffman (second from right) and her girlfriend chat with
American soldiers at the USO in New York City.

Ogawa at the Poston, Arizona, camp wrote her librarian friend, Clara Breed, "This camp is so far away from civilization that it makes me feel as if I was a convict who is not allowed to see anyone." A year later, she wrote, "That feeling of sorrow and emptiness in my tummy comes back to me every time I think of how I left San Diego."

"This camp is so far away from civilization that it makes me feel as if I was a convict who is not allowed to see anyone."

— Louise Ogawa, teenager

African American teenagers faced a different color barrier. In 1943 Martin Luther King Jr., fourteen, entered a high school speech contest in Georgia. In his speech, he said, "Black America still wears chains. . . . Even winners of our highest honors face the class color bar." He described a concert given by famous singer Marian Anderson in front of the Lincoln Memorial in Washington, D.C. A crowd of 75,000 people listened. Then he said, "Miss Anderson may not as yet spend the night in any good hotel. . . . If freedom is good for any, it is good for all."

Martin Luther King Jr. won the speech contest. But

A crowd of 75,000 heard Marian Anderson sing at the Lincoln Memorial.

on the bus home, he and his teacher had to give up their seats to white passengers. After standing for ninety miles, Martin said, "It was the angriest I have ever been in my life."

The next summer, he worked on a Connecticut tobacco farm. He wrote his father, "All the white people here are very nice. We go to any place we want and sit anywhere we want to."

When Martin Luther King Jr. was fourteen, he gave a speech about Marian Anderson.

WARTIME HIT PARADE

Your Hit Parade, a popular radio show, played each week's top songs. One of the biggest wartime hits was "White Christmas" by Irving Berlin. Others were:

"God Bless America"

"I'll Be Home for Christmas"

"Don't Sit under the Apple Tree with Anyone Else but Me"

"Comin' in on a Wing and a Prayer"

"Good-bye, Mama, I'm Off to Yokohama"

"The Last Time I Saw Paris"

"The White Cliffs of Dover"

Mara Hart and her sister made a game out of *Your Hit Parade.* "I would introduce Kitty, and she'd be the famous performer, singing that week's songs."

CHAPTER SIX

THE WAR ENDS

...we here highly resolve that these dead shall not have died in vain...

REMEMBER DEC. 7th!

"There were throngs of people embracing and crying and screaming. . . . what a glorious time to be alive!

—Jeannette Meyer, nineteen, Omaha, Nebraska, VJ (Victory in Japan) Day, 1945

★ ★

Mara Hart was in music class on April 12, 1945, when she heard that President Roosevelt had died. Her class immediately sang "America the Beautiful." Since Roosevelt had been in office for twelve years, he was the only president many children had known.

On May 8, 1945, German troops surrendered, and the war ended in Europe. It was called VE (Victory in Europe) Day. People danced in the streets when they heard about the surrender. But the war continued in Asia.

On August 6, 1945, the United States dropped an atomic bomb on Hiroshima, Japan, killing 140,000 people. Never before had such a terrible weapon been used against human beings. Three days later, on August 9, 1945, a second atomic bomb destroyed Nagasaki, Japan, killing 74,000 people. Many more died later from radiation poisoning caused by the bomb.

On August 14, 1945, Japan surrendered. Bob Jones, ten, was

The mushroom cloud of an atomic bomb rose over Nagasaki, Japan, on August 9, 1945.

Americans in New York City celebrated Japan's surrender
and the end of the war.

the first in his family to read the newspaper headlines that told of
the surrender. He raced inside to tell everyone. People all over the
United States celebrated on VJ Day. In Massachusetts kids
marched up and down neighborhood streets, banging spoons on
pots and pans.

Some people felt joy mixed with sadness at the news. "Not
everybody came home," said Martha Hoffman, then twenty. Her
sister's husband had died in the war. Martha's mother had lost most
of her Jewish relatives in Russia.

A Letter about Death

The war didn't end soon enough for Robert Raymond's brother Jack. In 1944 Robert, fourteen, read the official telegram, "a letter about death": "The Secretary of War asked that I assure you of his deep sympathy in the loss of your brother, Sgt. Enoch [Jack] W. Raymond....He was killed two [the second of] August in Italy."

Robert was devastated. "My anger at God that night was very real and intense," he said. "I [talked to] him long and hard about permitting wars and especially about letting one's brother be killed."

But World War II was over. In Georgia, Florence Fleming's first thoughts were of food: "Now we can have all the bubble gum we want, and ice cream won't taste like cold chalk anymore!" And Dot Chastney, twelve, would finally get her two-wheeled bicycle.

> *"Now . . . ice cream won't taste like cold chalk anymore!"*
> —*Florence Flemming*

★ ★ ★ ★

After the War

While dancing at the USO in New York City, Martha Hoffman had met and fallen in love with an American sailor. When he came home after the war, the young couple married and moved in with Martha's parents.

In 1944 Congress had passed the G.I. Bill. It paid for the education of people in the armed forces. Because of this, Martha's new husband went to college. So did many other veterans.

Martha Hoffman married her navy sweetheart, Leon Moorin. They met at a USO dance.

Families and friends greet sailors returning at the end of the war.

Some young people had married quickly before soldiers went overseas. Others married as soon as they returned. Some wounded veterans had to explain to their girlfriends or families that they had lost a limb or worse. Fathers often came home to children who didn't know them.

★ ★ ★ ★

THE STORY CONTINUES

World War II children grew up, married, and had families. Leroy Anderson married Jody Rhoads, who as a child had played commandos in her barnyard. Leroy became a professor of sociology and Asian studies. Jody worked as a medical technician, teacher, organist, and writer.

Sammy's poppa, Dr. Reuben Berman, came home safely. Sammy and his brother David became doctors, like their father. Bob Jones joined the air force, went to college on the G.I. Bill, and became an engineer. Robert Raymond worked as a public health officer on Indian reservations.

Mara Hart, who huddled in the dark with her sister and grandmother during air raid drills, became an English teacher, writer, and mother. All six of Marialyse Hager's brothers came home. Marjorie Boger Greek remained lifelong friends with the English girl, Vina, who lived with Marjorie's family during the war.

Dorinda Makanaonalani became a psychotherapist. She wrote a book about Pearl Harbor and often talks to children about the harmful effects of war.

TELEVISION

Philo Farnsworth, who made modern television possible, lived near Leroy Anderson's Idaho home. In 1947 the United States had 6,000 television sets. That number jumped to 100,000 in 1948, then to 7 million sets in 1953. By the 1980s, people had more television sets than bathtubs. In the twenty-first century, television is everywhere.

★ ★ ★ ★

DIVIDED BY RACE

Americans of different races had served their country bravely, fighting
side by side. At home, men and women of many races had worked
together in war factories. But after the war, America remained a
nation divided by race.

In college, Martin Luther King Jr. continued to write about equal
rights—jobs, education, safety, voting. He became a minister and a
great civil rights leader. He was killed by a white gunman in 1968.
Martin Luther King Jr.'s birthday, January 15, is a national holiday.

The Japanese American camps finally closed. Relocation had cost
many residents their jobs, homes, and possessions. For many years,
Jeanne Wakatsuki couldn't talk about her childhood experiences at
Manzanar. She later wrote a book about it.

★ ★ ★ ★

GROWING UP WITHOUT A FATHER

Because of the war, many children grew up without their fathers. In 1951
Susan Johnson, six, studied photos of her father, who had died in the
war. "My father was just a picture. I knew that my grandmother loved
him by the way she touched his picture. She gave *me* a deep, deep love
for him."

As the child of a WWII soldier,
Susan was also able to go to
college on the G.I. Bill. She
became a psychotherapist. Years
later, Susan found the place
where her father had died. She
placed flowers at a memorial wall
in Luxembourg. She and her

*"My father was just a
picture. I knew that
my grandmother loved
him by the way she
touched his picture."*
—*Susan Johnson*

LIVES LOST IN WORLD WAR II

Americans who served in World War II: 16 million

American soldiers killed: 405,399

Japanese killed by the atomic bomb:

Hiroshima 140,000

Nagasaki 74,000

Killed in Hitler's concentration camps: 11 million

family held a funeral service to honor him at Arlington National Cemetery. "Things are left undone in war," she said. Susan Johnson Hadler and a coauthor wrote a book about American war orphans.

★ ★ ★ ★

IN THE WAR TOGETHER

During World War II, young people did lots of ordinary things, like play baseball, deliver newspapers, jump rope. But they also did real war work. They collected scrap metal, tended victory gardens, and did other jobs kids didn't usually do. "Everyone felt we were in the war together, to win," said Jody Rhoads.

Movies, books, and radio shows made battles seem exciting. Many youngsters even thought playing war was fun—until someone didn't come home. When loved ones died, children grew silent, sad, and sometimes afraid. They learned that war could separate families. Many children had to grow up fast.

After December 7, 1941, the country's rallying cry was, "Remember Pearl Harbor!" Those who lived during this time never forgot. As children, and later, as adults, they found that World War II changed their lives forever.

ACTIVITIES

Study a Historical Photograph

Always ask questions when you study a photograph, painting, or drawing. The answers tell you what you can't see. Who are the people? What are they doing? What are they thinking and feeling? What information does the picture give you?

Photographs of the children you learned about appear in this book. Most of the pictures are black and white since color photographs didn't become common until later in the twentieth century. Study the photograph on the cover. What do you notice about the roller skates the girls are wearing? Why do you think the girls are sharing one pair of skates? How do their roller skates differ from ones you may have? How are the girls' clothes and hairstyles different from the way girls you know dress and wear their hair?

Make a list of what you see. Compare your list with others. Working together, write a short paragraph about what you and others in your group think the photograph tells us. Follow these steps with other illustrations and photographs in this book.

Be a Movie Reviewer

Rent or borrow a movie from the World War II era, such as *Mrs. Miniver* or *Thirty Seconds over Tokyo*. Write what you think of it and how life in the film compares to life today.

Just for Fun!

Study chapter four. Then make a list of ten things young people did for fun during WWII. Include games, like stickball, and toys, like Slinkies® and Silly Putty®. Make a list of ten things you do for fun. Include the most popular games and toys. Compare your lists with someone else.

"Use It Up, Wear It Out, Make It Do, or Do Without!"

During WWII, rationing helped conserve important goods. Reusing scrap metal, rubber, newspaper, even kitchen grease, helped the war effort. In modern times, people recycle glass, plastic, metal, paper, and computer parts. Some people put their yard waste and their fruit and vegetable scraps into compost piles. This helps the environment.

Look around your bedroom, kitchen, classroom, or some other common place. Make a list of items that can be recycled.

Think of a slogan like the one above—words that will help people remember to recycle. For example, "Recycle Today for a Better Tomorrow" or "Let Worms Do the Job," for people who compost with earthworms.

Try a Wartime Recipe

Wartime recipes had names like Victory Cake and Washington Pie and were published in newspapers, magazines, and cookbooks. The recipes suggested substitutes for ingredients in short supply. In the recipe below for Red Rover cookies, honey takes the place of sugar. Families might have grown the carrots in their victory garden. (Red Rover was also the name of a popular game children played.)

Red Rovers

(makes 3 dozen cookies)

2 cups flour	2 cups quick oatmeal
2 teaspoons baking powder	1 cup raisins
¼ teaspoon baking soda	½ cup shortening
¼ teaspoon salt	1 cup raw carrots, grated
½ teaspoon cinnamon	1 cup honey
½ teaspoon nutmeg	2 eggs, well beaten

Sift flour and measure. Blend with baking powder, soda, salt, cinnamon, and nutmeg, and resift. Add oatmeal and raisins and mix well. Blend in the shortening. Stir in carrots, then add honey and eggs. Add to flour mixture, a little at a time. Mix well. Drop by teaspoonsful onto a greased baking sheet and bake in a moderate oven (350°F) for about 20–25 minutes.

SOURCE NOTES

2 Eleanor Roosevelt, quoted in the *Washington Post*, July 19, 1940, 1.

7 Dorinda Makanaonalani Nicholson, *Pearl Harbor Child: A Child's View of Pearl Harbor—From Attack to Peace* (Kansas City, MO: Woodson House Publishing, 1998), 15.

7, 8 Ibid., 19.

8 Ginger, quoted in B. Z. Leonard, ed., *Ginger's Diary 1941*, December 7, 1941, <http://www.gingersdiary.com/diary.html>.

8 Franklin D. Roosevelt, quoted in Peter Jennings and Todd Brewster, *The Century* (New York: Doubleday, 1998), 230.

8 Penny Coleman, *Rosie the Riveter* (New York: Crown, 1995), 69.

10 Ibid., 66.

11 Robert G. Raymond, *Scouting, Cavorting & Other World War II Memories: A Young Sioux Indian Lad's Memories of World War II* (Billings, MT: Benchmark Printers-Bookbinders, 1994), 48.

12 David S. Johnson Jr., quoted in Susan Johnson Hadler and Ann Bennett Mix, *Lost in the Victory* (Denton, TX: University of North Texas Press, 1998), 216.

13 Jeanne Wakatsuki Houston and James D. Houston, *Farewell to Manzanar* (New York: Bantam, 1995), 9.

15 Marialyse Hager, quoted in Lori Cox, "What Did You Do in the War?" *Nebraska History*, Winter 1991, 229.

15 Ginger, quoted in Leonard, December 31, 1941.

17 Sammy Berman, quoted in Ruth Berman, ed., *Dear Poppa, The World War II Berman Family Letters* (St. Paul, MN: Minnesota Historical Press, 1997), 102–103.

17 Ibid., 149.

18 Bob Jones, interviewed by author, Cardiff-by-the-Sea, CA, March 5, 2001.

19 Jack Raymond, quoted in Raymond, 94.

19 Ann Toplovich, "The Tennessean's War: Life on the Home Front," *Tennessee Historical Quarterly*, Spring 1992, 67.

20 Florence Fleming Corley, "Recollections of a Georgia Grammar School Girl, December 7, 1941 to September 2, 1945" (paper presented at "A Personal Recollection of the Homefront of World War II in the South," a symposium at Georgia State University in Atlanta, Georgia, May 1–2, 1992), 4.

20 Susan L. Gordon, "Home Front Tennessee: The World War II Experience," *Tennessee Historical Quarterly*, Spring 1992, 15.

20–21 Jody Rhoads Anderson, quoted in C. Leroy Anderson, Yunosuke Ohkura, and Joanne R. Anderson, *No Longer Silent* (Missoula, MT: Pictorial Histories Publishing Co., 1995), 195.

21 Coleman, 9.

21 Nicholson, 41.

22 John E. Smith, quoted in Tom Brokaw, *The Greatest Generation Speaks* (New York: Random House, 1999), 206–208.

22 Corley, 2.

23 Mara Hart, telephone interview by author, July 20, 2001.

24 Louise Ogawa, quoted in Donald H. Estes and Matthew T. Estes, "Letters from Camp: Poston—The First Year," *Journal of the West*, April 1999, 23.

25 Jeanne Wakatsuki, quoted in Houston, 40.

25 Ibid., 33.

27 Bruce Smith, *The History of Little Orphan Annie* (New York: Ballantine, 1982), 50.

27 Nicholson, 41.

28 Martin Luther King Jr., *The Papers of Martin Luther King, Jr.*, volume 1, *Called to Serve, January 1929–June 1951*, Clayborne Carson, ed. (Berkeley: University of California Press, 1992), 103.

28 Ibid., 107.

28 Gordon, 15.

28 Jody Rhoads Anderson, telephone interview by author, July 2, 2001.

29 Robert Joe Stout, "Lend Him a Hand!" *Southwest Review*, Summer 1984, 264.

29 Ibid., 262.

30 Barbara M. Tucker, "Agricultural Workers in World War II: The Reserve Army of Children, Black Americans, and Jamaicans," *Agricultural History*, Winter 1994, 56.

31 Mara Hart, telephone interview by author, July 20, 2001.

33 Coleman, 51.

34 Hisako Watanabe, quoted in Estes, 31.

34–35 Michael O. Tunnell and George W. Chilcoat, *The Children of Topaz* (New York: Holiday House, 1996), 18.

35 Mara Hart, July 20, 2001.

37 Martha Hoffman Witz, telephone interview by author, July 11, 2001.

37 Ibid.

38 King, 103.

38–39 C. Leroy Anderson, 10–11.

39 Marc McCutcheon, *Everyday Life from Prohibition through World War II* (Cincinnati, OH: Writer's Digest Books, 1995), 193.

39 William M. Tuttle Jr. *Daddy's Gone to War: The Second World War in the Lives of America's Children* (New York: Oxford University Press, 1993), 149.

40 McCutcheon, 196.

40 Tony Augarde, ed., *The Oxford Dictionary of Modern Quotations (*Oxford: Oxford University Press, 1991), 6.

41 Neal Shine, quoted in Jennings, 242–243.

42 Gordon, 7.

42 Jeanne Wakatsuki, quoted in Houston, 109.

43 Mara Hart, July 20, 2001.

45 Nancy Potter, quoted in Students in the Honors English Program, South Kingston High School, *What Did You Do in the War, Grandma?* (Providence, RI: Rhode Island Historical Society, 1989), 7.

45 Raymond, 59.

46 Nancy Potter, quoted in Students in the Honors English Program, 7.

46 Mary Wilderhain, ibid., 47.

47 Martha Hoffman Witz, July 11, 2001.

48 Louise Ogawa, quoted in Estes, 23.

48 King, 110.

49 Ibid., 110.

49 Ibid., 112.

49 Mara Hart, July 20, 2001.

51 Jeannette Meyer Davis, quoted in Cox, 241.

52 Martha Hoffman Witz, July 11, 2001.

53 Raymond, 119.

53 Ibid., 120.

53 Corley, 9.

56 Susan Johnson Hadler, telephone interview by author, July 19, 2001.

57 Ibid.

57 Jody Rhoads Anderson, telephone interview by author, July 2, 2001.

59 Coleman, 9.

SELECTED BIBLIOGRAPHY

Anderson, C. Leroy, Yunosuke Ohkura, and Joanne R. Anderson. *No Longer Silent*. Missoula, MT: Pictorial Histories Publishing Co., 1995.

Berman, Ruth, ed. *Dear Poppa, The World War II Berman Family Letters*. St. Paul, MN: Minnesota Historical Press, 1997.

Brokaw, Tom. *The Greatest Generation Speaks*. New York: Random House, 1999.

Coleman, Penny. *Rosie the Riveter*. New York: Crown, 1995.

Hadler, Susan Johnson, and Ann Bennett Mix. *Lost in the Victory*. Denton, TX: University of North Texas Press, 1998.

Houston, Jeanne Wakatsuki, and James D. Houston. *Farewell to Manzanar*. New York: Bantam, 1995.

Jennings, Peter, and Todd Brewster. *The Century*. New York: Doubleday, 1998.

Leonard, B. Z., ed. *Ginger's Diary 1941*. September 14, 2001.
    <http://www.gingersdiary.com/diary.html>.

Lingeman, Richard. *Don't You Know There's a War On?* New York: G. P. Putnams, 1970.

Litoff, Judy Barrett, and David C. Smith. *Since You Went Away: World War II Letters from American Women on the Home Front*. Lawrence, KS: University Press of Kansas, 1991.

McCutcheon, Marc. *Everyday Life from Prohibition through World War II*. Cincinnati, OH: Writer's Digest Books, 1995.

Murphy, Margot. *Wartime Meals: How to Plan Them, How to Buy Them, How to Cook Them*. New York: Greenburg, 1942.

Nicholson, Dorinda Makanaonalani. *Pearl Harbor Child: A Child's View of Pearl Harbor — From Attack to Peace*. Kansas City, MO: Woodson House Publishing, 1998.

Parsons, Farnell. *Prelude, Conflict and Aftermath: A Bibliography of World War II Children's Literature*. St. Louis, MO: Farnell Parsons, 1999.

Raymond, Robert G. *Scouting, Cavorting & Other World War II Memories: A Young Sioux Indian Lad's Memories of World War II*. Billings, MT: Benchmark Printers-Bookbinders, 1994.

Students in the Honors English Program, South Kingston High School. *What Did You Do in the War, Grandma?* Providence, RI: Rhode Island Historical Society, 1989.

Tunnell, Michael O., and George W. Chilcoat. *The Children of Topaz*. New York: Holiday House, 1996.

Tuttle, William M. Jr. *Daddy's Gone to War: The Second World War in the Lives of America's Children*. New York: Oxford University Press, 1993.

West, Elliot. *Growing Up in Twentieth Century America*. Westport, CT: Greenwood Press, 1996.

Witz, Martha. *Step by Step*. Encinitas, CA: Martha Witz, 1991.

Young, Peter. *The World Almanac of World War II*. New York: World Almanac, 1986.

FURTHER READING AND WEBSITES

Banim, Lisa. *American Dreams*. New York: Silver Moon, 1993.

Bauer, Marion Dane. *Rain of Fire*. New York: Clarion, 1983.

Chaikin, Miriam. *Friends Forever*. Lincoln, NE: iUniverse.com, 2001.

Coerr, Elanor. *Sadako*. New York: Puffin, 1993.

Cormier, Robert. *Other Bells for Us to Ring*. New York: Delacorte, 1990.

Cutler, Jane. *My Wartime Summers*. New York: Farrar, Strauss & Giroux, 1994.

Department of the Navy. *Naval Historical Center*. http://www.history.navy.mil/index.html.

Garner, Eleanor Ramrath. *Eleanor's Story*. Atlanta, GA: Peachtree Publishers, 1999.

Giff, Patricia Reilly. *Lily's Crossing*. New York: Delacorte, 1997.

Glassman, Judy. *The Morning Glory War*. New York: Dutton, 1990.

Hahn, Mary Downing. *Stepping on the Cracks*. Boston: Clarion Books, 1991.

The History Place. *World War Two in Europe*.
   http://www.historyplace.com/worldwar2/timeline/ww2time.htm.

King, David C. *World War II Days: Discover the Past with Exciting Projects, Games, Activities, and Recipes*. New York: John Wiley & Sons, 2000.

Knight, Eric Mowbray. *Lassie Come-Home*. New York: Dell, 1940.

Lazo, Caroline. *Harry Truman*. Minneapolis, MN: Lerner Publications Company, 2003.

Lowry, Lois. *Autumn Street*. Boston: Houghton Mifflin, 1980.

———. *Number the Stars*. Boston: Houghton Mifflin, 1989.

McPherson, Stephanie Sammartino. *TV's Forgotten Hero: The Story of Philo Farnsworth*. Minneapolis: Lerner Publications Company, 1996.

Mochizuki, Ken. *Baseball Saved Us*. New York: Lee & Low, 1993.

———. *Heroes*. New York: Lee & Low, 1995.

O'Connor, Barbara. *The Soldier's Voice: The Story of Ernie Pyle*. Minneapolis, MN: Carolrhoda Books, Inc., 1996.

Paulsen, Gary. *The Cookcamp*. New York: Orchard, 1991.

Roberts, Jeremy. *Franklin D. Roosevelt*. Minneapolis, MN: Lerner Publications Company, 2003.

Savin, Marcia. *The Moon Bridge*. New York: Scholastic, 1992.

Say, Allen. *Home of the Brave*. Boston: Houghton Mifflin, 2002.

Stevenson, James. *Don't You Know There's a War On?* New York: Greenwillow, 1992.

Students in the Honors English Program, South Kingston High School. *What Did You Do in the War, Grandma?* http://www.stg.brown.edu/projects/WWII_Women/tocCS.html.

Uchida, Yoshiko. *The Invisible Thread: An Autobiography*. New York: Beech Tree Books, 1995.

INDEX